How GRACE became Amazing

SANDY RECKERT-REUSING

Illustrated by Cynthia Ramirez Herrick

How GRACE became Amazing

Interior Image Credit: Cynthia Ramirez Herrick

WestBow Press books may be ordered through booksellers or by contacting:

WestBow Press
A Division of Thomas Nelson & Zondervan
1663 Liberty Drive
Bloomington, IN 47403
www.westbowpress.com
1 (866) 928-1240

ISBN: 978-1-9736-3862-9 (sc)
ISBN: 978-1-9736-3863-6 (e)

Library of Congress Control Number: 2018912657

Print information available on the last page.

WestBow Press rev. date: 11/7/2018

WestBow
PRESS®
A DIVISION OF THOMAS NELSON
& ZONDERVAN

From the Author

In a sense, we are all butterflies in a chrysalis.

God is always working in us and for us

as he transforms our lives.

And it's that perfect moment — that amazing day —

when we will burst forth, and on wings of grace, fly!

Story inspired by Jeanie Reckert.

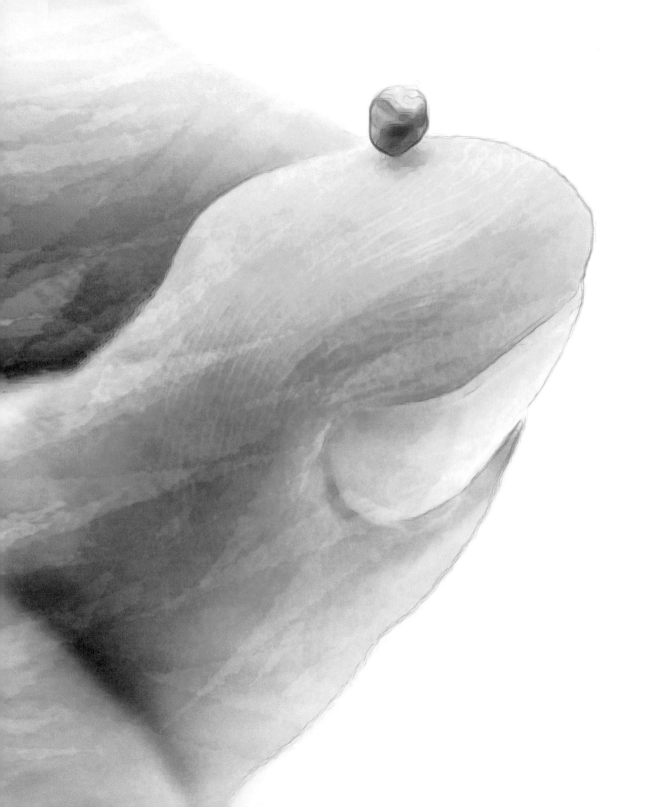

A mustard seed is usually not so *amazing*,
But that is exactly how Grace came to be.

She was the size of a mustard seed SITTING ON A

milkweed.

And on that milkweed she felt right at home,

Because Grace was never really

alone.

She was very hungry so she ate and ate,

until she grew from small to

great.

GRACE BECAME A CHUBBY CATERPILLAR
AND WAS ALSO QUITE SHY.
SHE TUCKED IN HER HEAD AND HID HER

eyes.

Her lime and black stripes were a sight to behold.

Although she was humble, her story had to be

told.

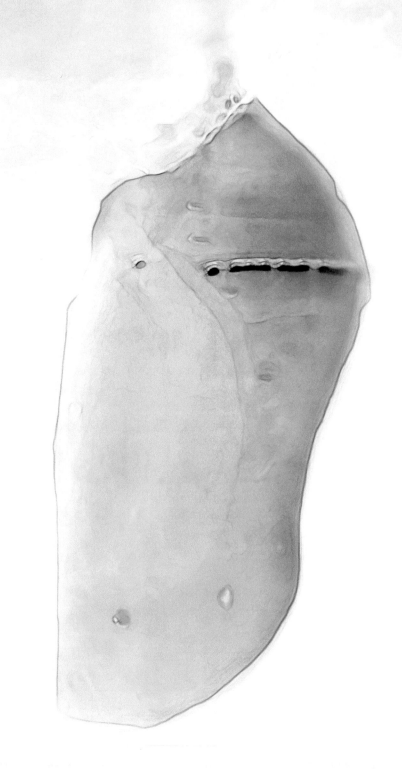

She formed a chrysalis — a blanket-type wrap,

and for 10 days she took a long

Nap.

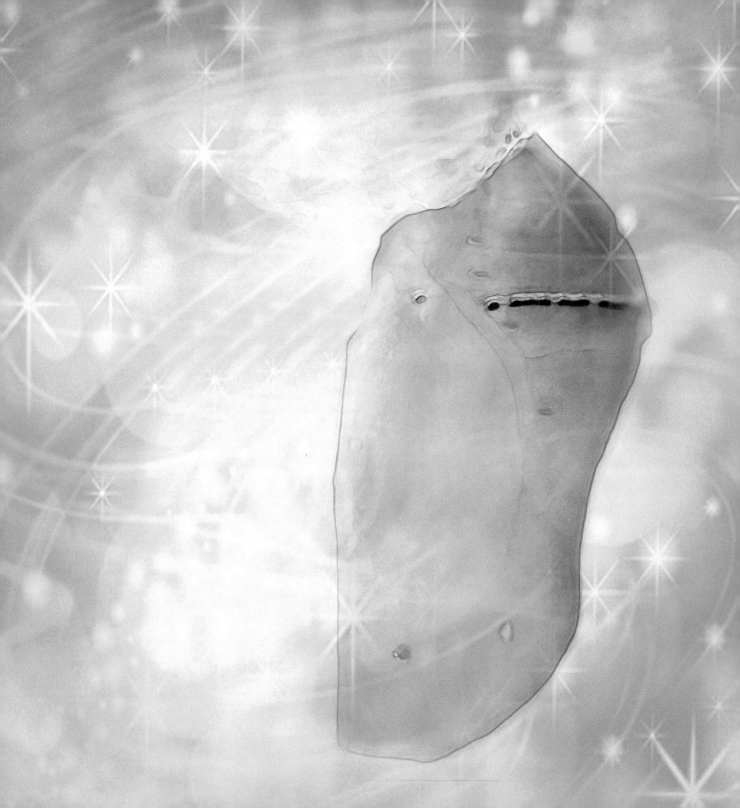

But what she was doing in there was beyond imagination.

For inside the chrysalis, Grace became a whole new

creation.

THE CHRYSALIS CHANGED FROM GREEN TO CLEAR.

WAS THIS THE SIGN HER TIME WAS

near?

LEGS FIRST AND THEN WINGS FROM THE CHRYSALIS SHE CAME.

THAT'S WHEN GRACE KNEW SHE'D NEVER BE THE

same.

THIS TIMID CATERPILLAR WAS SHY NO MORE.

SHE HAD A NEW LIFE AND HER SPIRIT COULD

soar.

AND DURING THAT DAY SHE EMERGED FROM THE DARK,

AND BECAME A BEAUTIFUL BUTTERFLY—A

monarch.

She spread her bright orange wings and took to the sky.

And with tears of joy, I whispered

goodbye.

For she was a gift—the handiwork
of the Lord our King.
He was the reason Grace became

amazing.

ABOUT THE AUTHOR

Sandy Recket-Reusing has been in the publications and communi-cations field for 36 years. Earlier in her career, she worked as a newspaper reporter, freelance writer and graphic designer. Currently, she oversees and guides the communications efforts as a senior director of marketing and communications at a prominent medical institution. Sandy's passion for finding "God in nature," led her to write How Grace Became Amazing. She also expresses her spirituality in her blog, called Meaningful Moments, which can be found at https://meaningfulmoments.blog. Sandy earned her Master of Arts in Writing and Graphic Design from the University of Baltimore in 1995. She earned her Bachelor of Arts in Journalism with a minor in Public Relations in 1985.

ABOUT THE ILLUSTRATOR

As a veteran visual designer, Cynthia Ramirez Herrick integrates digital technology with her creative visual arts background. Her expertise in illustration, graphic design and photography combined with her advertising degree from the University of Maryland, Cynthia has produced strong conceptual marketing materials for dozens of organizations and her photography has been recognized by National Geographic.

Printed in the United States
By Bookmasters